Designing Life's Celebrations

Photography by Monica Buck

RIZZOLI
NEW YORK

New York Paris London Milan

Designing Life's Celebrations

DeJuan Stroud

with Debra Stroud

Foreword by Dorothea and Jon Bon Jovi

For Rob, Molly,
Emily, and George,
and for Oliver

Foreword
By Dorothea and Jon Bon Jovi

We first became aware of DeJuan Stroud's floral arrangements in 1997, when a dear friend of ours told us about a beautiful arrangement she had seen in a local tea shop in New Jersey. We happened to stop by the shop later that week and saw another sweet arrangement there, accompanied by a business card. Our friend's passing mention of those flowers was such a small thing, but it was the beginning of a wonderful relationship.

We began working with DeJuan on a fundraiser for Doug Flutie's Foundation for Autism that we were hosting in our home, and we quickly realized how talented DeJuan was. He is that rare person who listens and completely understands what his clients are trying to achieve, and he creates the most striking spaces. For that evening, we decided at the last minute to paint the dance floor red! Our friends had an incredible time, and we raised a lot of money for a really good cause.

DeJuan has done so many events and created so many floral designs for us since then, from big birthday bashes to small yet stunning arrangements for Valentine's Day. DeJuan's vision and passion for his work come through in everything he does. When our children were younger he would decorate our house for Christmas with topiaries of toy soldiers and garlands spelling the words Peace and Love that we still use to this day.

What we love most about DeJuan is that his vision is our vision—he creates what his clients want, not what he wants. As you look through this gorgeous book you will see many different party spaces and floral arrangements, but they all have the following qualities in common: they are tasteful, elegant, and fun, which is exactly how we would describe DeJuan. Together we have had so much fun doing these parties. He is sweet and has a good sense of humor, and he doesn't take his work so seriously that it becomes overbearing. Our guests always ask how we create such incredible parties; they think we must have a million meetings about details, and planning, but honestly, after so many years DeJuan knows exactly what we want even before we do, because he has been listening all that time.

A few years ago, when we started the pilot program for our community restaurant, JBJ Soul Kitchen, we were using a church gymnasium in Red Bank, New Jersey, as our dining area. We wanted to create a space that looked like a restaurant, one where people in need could eat with dignity. We called DeJuan, who, without hesitating, offered to help and donate whatever we needed to transform that gymnasium into a gracious space. By that time, DeJuan had moved his thriving business to New York City and was very busy. But every week he and his wife, Debra, would drive down and put together the most gorgeous centerpieces—arrangements so spectacular that diners would pose in front of them to have their pictures taken.

We have watched DeJuan Stroud grow from being a small florist in Little Silver, New Jersey, to an event-design star in New York City. He has done that through hard work and dedication to his craft. He is a true artist, and we are proud to call him our friend.

OPPOSITE: Peonies, amaryllis, and roses in varied shades of coral come together for a striking monochromatic bouquet.

Introduction

It was a perfect late summer Sunday afternoon brightened by golden sunshine, yellow roses, lace tablecloths, a multi-tiered cake, stacks of gifts, and lots and lots of laughter from relatives and friends who had come from all over the South. I was eight years old, and my paternal grandparents were celebrating their fiftieth wedding anniversary. Early on the morning of the party, my grandmother had asked me to follow her through the garden with a pail of water. As she cut flowers, she handed them to me to put into the pail. Next, I watched as she arranged slender branches of mock orange foliage, camellia leaves, deep yellow roses, and pale yellow zinnias in ceramic and china vases and placed them throughout her house.

While my grandmother had ordered a few special arrangements from the florist in town for the main tables, I much preferred her own arrangements. To me, her bouquets seemed more thoughtful and more perfectly suited to the interiors of the red farmhouse. The flowers made the house seem dressed up for a party. That afternoon, standing on the sidelines of the dining room with my brother, Chris, I watched as my grandparents, my father, and my father's six sisters greeted guests, and I saw the joy that they took in celebrating that happy occasion. Looking back, I think that day inspired my deep love for flowers, as well as serving as the foundation of my belief that all of life's milestones should be marked by celebrations.

I grew up in a small town in South Alabama. As a teenager, I worked in a flower shop for several summers. There I was exposed to the retail flower business for the first time, including the mechanics of old-school floral arranging, and decorating for events, such as teas, receptions, and weddings. After graduating from college, I moved with my wife, Debra, to New Orleans, where I became a stockbroker. Three years later, with two children in tow, we relocated to the Northeast, where I worked on Wall Street. During that time, I never lost my love for

OPPOSITE: In a room with pale gray walls, I selected garden roses, cyclamen, and sweet peas in shades of pink to play off the hot pink upholstery of the chairs.

flowers and entertaining. I especially enjoyed helping friends with small weddings and parties. From arranging flowers in church to decorating a friend's birthday party, I kept practicing those skills I had first learned back at that flower shop in Alabama.

A fter ten years, I decided to leave Wall Street and get back to doing what I loved. Debra and I started an event design business in our basement in Little Silver, New Jersey, and shortly thereafter moved the business to New York City. That was twenty years ago. As the business grew, we progressed from providing mainly floral arrangements to handling full-scale decor design for both social and corporate events. Today, Debra and I manage a team that creates the decor for some of the most beautiful events in the country.

Over the years, clients have often asked me to guide them in entertaining at home, and friends and family have also sought my advice on how to make their holidays and parties more distinctive. While I primarily decorate large-scale events, many of the principles I follow can be applied to the more intimate scale of home entertaining: make it welcoming; make it beautiful; pay attention to details.

I wrote this book to share what I've learned and to show how details can enhance an experience and set it apart. When you are designing your table, I encourage you to examine the elements; notice color palettes; consider composition and placement; and pay attention to the surroundings. Through the parties featured in this book, I explore many of the details associated with home entertaining. From the curvy vine of a clematis to a baby artichoke weighting a napkin, each element has been carefully selected to provide balance and counterbalance.

OPPOSITE: These four photographs are from the wedding of my daughter, Emily. She carried a bouquet of cream Vendela roses, green ornithogalum, Iceberg roses, and variegated hosta leaves. The room was set with long tables in the shape of the letter E in tribute to Emily and her husband, Eric. Flower arrangements of several different styles were placed down the lengths of the tables; a Venetian vase held a simple bouquet of Sterling roses. The floral arrangements were all low, and candles added height to the tables.

In the course of a year, we all have days that are routine and days that are exciting. I may not remember last Wednesday, but I remember everything about the days that my children were born. The same can be said about holidays and special occasions—some we remember; some we don't. Let's change that. Bring out your prettiest linens; fill the room with candles and turn off all the lights; create gorgeous floral centerpieces; move your table to a different spot. All these things take effort, but when people make an effort, an unforgettable occasion is guaranteed.

I t's important to note that making a celebration memorable doesn't have to mean making it formal and fussy. Years and years ago, a dinner party at home was a stiff, prescribed meal on a table set with the perfunctory white tablecloth, china, silver, and crystal. All the men were in suits and ties and all the women in dresses and high heels. Thankfully, just as dress codes have relaxed, those rigid parameters for being a "proper" host and hostess have changed, allowing a fresh take on entertaining. One of my favorite meals in recent years took place when the in-laws of my daughter Emily came to spend Thanksgiving with us. On the usually dull night before the holiday, Jo Anne and Will arrived from Maine with everything for a classic New England lobster dinner. They unpacked an enormous pot, a big cooler of lobsters, a crock of baked beans, and three blueberry pies. Lobster bibs, claw crackers, picks, and small ramekins for butter showed that they had planned carefully. Jo Anne had even printed a menu that included a funny poem written for the occasion. We set up a wooden table in our foyer, rolled out oilcloth, and lit the whole scene with hurricane lamps. It was a meal that I will never forget.

A client once asked me what I thought about the ephemeral quality of event design. She recognized that a lot of work and resources are expended for a short period of time, and asked if I felt that what I do is wasteful. I told her that my goal is to create a setting that gives people lasting memories. The happiness you give to guests at a celebration and the warmth felt around a holiday table are of immeasurable worth. When you bring beauty, care, and attention to an occasion, you mark the moment—for a lifetime.

PART I

Celebrations

An Elegant Dinner in Greenwich
• Romance at Home • Just Desserts
• Contemporary Loft Dinner

An Elegant Dinner in Greenwich

One of my favorite parties from the first few years of our business was done completely in red. Flowers, tablecloths, chairs, lighting, and even the dance floor were all fire-engine red for this casual summer party, and it looked spectacular. In the years since, I have used a single bold color to decorate everything from casual parties to corporate dinners to dressy galas. Employing the power of just one color continues to be a sensational approach to design and was the driving force behind the look I created for the elegant dinner party that a Greenwich couple gave to celebrate moving into their new home. I chose pink—ranging in shades from soft, almost pastel pink to bold deep fuchsia—for the flowers so that they would stand out against the extraordinary chartreuse-lacquered walls of the dining room.

The couple's chic dining table with its top of silver leaf inlay was an excellent foil for the show-off flowers that I wanted to use, so no tablecloth was needed—just a show-stopping centerpiece. I decided to give the table an abundant look with four lush bouquets. The largest arrangement included Yves Piaget garden roses, South American roses, ranunculus, anemones, mini Phalaenopsis orchids, and cattleya orchids. Another bouquet included Yves Piaget garden roses, vanda orchids, and peonies, while the two smallest bouquets were of ranunculus and peonies. The flowers were arranged in square mirrored vases that seemed to fade away, keeping all attention on the magnificent saturated colors.

Even though pink was the focus of my design, I included gold accents to lend warmth to the tabletop and to play off the gold elements that were already in the room. I dressed up the place settings with charger plates with wide pebbled gold rims, and white linen napkins with gold-and-silver embroidered borders were held by interlocking gold rings. Vermeil flatware added more warm gold. With so much color, texture, and detail already on the table, I wanted the glassware to be exceptional so that it would add to the design instead of being

PRECEDING PAGE: Intense pink flowers on the table and on the sideboards made the room seem filled with flowers. OPPOSITE: As a lovely way to bring more color to the table, a vivid pink and burgundy cattleya orchid was placed on every other napkin.

Small photographs of the clients' artwork were encased in clear Lucite, inscribed with the guests' names, and taken home at the end of the evening to be used as paperweights.

overlooked. Champagne glasses that were heavily embellished with a gold Edwardian design, gold-banded amber water glasses, and etched wineglasses with gold rims held their own on this stunning table.

Five tall tapers in crystal candlesticks contributed the height needed to give the centerpiece presence in the room and were a quiet complement to the vivid flowers. Down below, oversized votive candles of heavy gold and silver Murano glass spoke to the gold of the place settings and the silver leaf of the table inlay.

Lastly, bouquets of pink flowers extended dynamic color to the perimeter of the room. We filled the sideboards with masses of orchids, and the mantels were filled with roses. With its bold pink statements, the dining room was ready for a memorable first party in the couple's new home.

PRECEDING PAGE, LEFT: The sideboards held luscious arrangements of Phalaenopsis orchids and mini Phalaenopsis orchids in bronze vases. PRECEDING PAGE, RIGHT: Candles lit, the dining room was ready for the arrival of the guests. FOLLOWING PAGES, FIRST PAGE, LEFT: Hot-pink anemones with their smooth petals were the perfect complement to the ruffled petals of the Yves Piaget roses. FIRST PAGE, RIGHT: I loved the way the pink flowers stood out against the chartreuse walls. SECOND PAGE, LEFT: This close-up of the table's centerpiece shows the layering of the color pink with hot-pink roses against fuchsia cattleya orchids, soft-pink ranunculus, and purple/pink mini Phalaenopsis orchids. SECOND PAGE, RIGHT: Antique brass vases played up the rich magenta tones of the vanda orchids.

Romance at Home

Designing the decor for my daughter's wedding was a unique experience for me. Having decorated countless weddings in twenty years of business, I often wondered what in the world I would do for Emily's big day. It turned out to be easier than I expected. Emily told me that she wanted "tons of flowers and candles, a romantic look, and nothing modern." She added that she would like the flowers to look like a bridal bouquet that I had designed for *Martha Stewart Weddings* magazine several years earlier. With that in mind, I filled the room with flowers and an abundance of candlelight, and we celebrated Emily and Eric's wedding.

Often when I speak to the parents of our brides and grooms after a wedding, they say that they wish they could experience the whole evening all over again. Debra and I felt the same way, so when Emily's in-laws came to our house for dinner a few months after she and Eric were married, I though it would be fun to relive the wedding dinner by setting the table with a scaled-down version of their wedding decor. To start, I placed full, romantic bouquets of hydrangea, David Austin roses, clematis, tea roses, anemones, passion vine, and amaryllis down the length of the table. Echoing the palette for Emily and Eric's wedding, the flowers were in soft tones of coral, cream, apricot, lavender, and blush. Myrtle topiaries added height to the design, and mercury-glass votive candles and tall taper candles in chunky glass holders supplied the candlelight that Emily loves. I chose not to use a tablecloth, because I liked the rich color of the mahogany table, but I did add a mirror runner to anchor the centerpiece elements and to reflect the candlelight.

When I decorate for a dinner party, I like to extend the decor to other places in the room. In this instance, I placed a tall conical ivy topiary and a large glass bowl of Seckel pears on a round table in a large bay window at the end of the dining room. I filled the mantel with pillar candles, votive candles, and bouquets of blush-toned roses in Venetian glass vases.

The overall effect of the flowers and candlelight was wonderfully romantic and reminded us of the magic of the wedding dinner. It was a perfect celebration of a perfect celebration.

OPPOSITE: The table was set with antique glassware and silverware, simple silver-bordered white china, natural linen napkins, and pretty place cards by the wedding calligrapher.

Mary

A petite bouquet
of three roses
was placed on a
beveled mirror for
added presence.

PREVIOUS PAGE, LEFT: The tines of the dessert forks held calligraphed place
cards. PREVIOUS PAGE, RIGHT: All set, the table had a lush, full look that
reminded us of the tables at Emily and Eric's wedding. FOLLOWING PAGE,
LEFT: Few things are more elegant than two or three stems of roses in a
graceful glass vase. FOLLOWING PAGE, RIGHT: For a scaled-down version
of this look, single blossoms of peonies, roses, and ranunculus could be
used instead of full bouquets. Here, flower-patterned vintage-style plates
ensured that the table looked special, even with fewer flowers.

Just Desserts

thoughtfully styled buffet can turn a casual gathering of friends into an event. In this instance, Debra and I hosted an informal post-concert dessert buffet for a group of twelve. While we were serving only a simple selection of cakes, cookies, and confections, we still wanted this gathering to feel special. Instead of using the dining room, we set up the buffet in the entrance hall, and we chose to use a glass-top table because the black-and-white marble floor beneath the table was an attractive background for the dessert display.

I started the buffet design by placing two large floral arrangements at the back of the table. I love colorful flowers, but for this table I wanted the flowers to be green and pale yellow, a combination that was striking against the pale gray walls of our entrance hall. Two flared faux concrete vases were filled with ornithogalum, Leucadendron, proteas, green carnations, pale yellow tea roses, viburnum, eucalyptus, pine, and western cedar. The use of several varieties of greenery and flowers with lots of texture gave an interesting, complex look to the arrangements, and their oversized scale drew attention to the buffet.

For presenting the desserts, I chose an assemblage of silver, glass, and glazed ceramic stands and platters at several different heights. An alternating line of white-and-taupe hemstitched linen dessert napkins, staggered rows of antique silver dessert forks, and stacks of hand-painted china plates gave a fin-de-siècle charm to the table, and a large chocolate snail was a one-off point of interest that made everyone smile. Guests weren't there to mark a special occasion, but it still felt like a celebration.

OPPOSITE: Arranged on the glass-top table, neatly ordered linen napkins and silver forks seemed to float. FOLLOWING PAGE, LEFT: Leucadendron, tea roses, ornithogalum, and viburnum were included in the green and pale yellow arrangements on the buffet. FOLLOWING PAGE, RIGHT: A flokati rug, which mimicked the texture of the coconut cake, was added for warmth on the chilly evening of the party. PAGE 42: When styling buffets, keep in mind that it is pleasing to the eye for the elements to be at different heights. Here, I used a pedestal bowl for candy, and a wooden box held macarons, as well as serving as a platform for a chocolate snail. PAGE 43: Colorful candies added a fun look to the buffet.

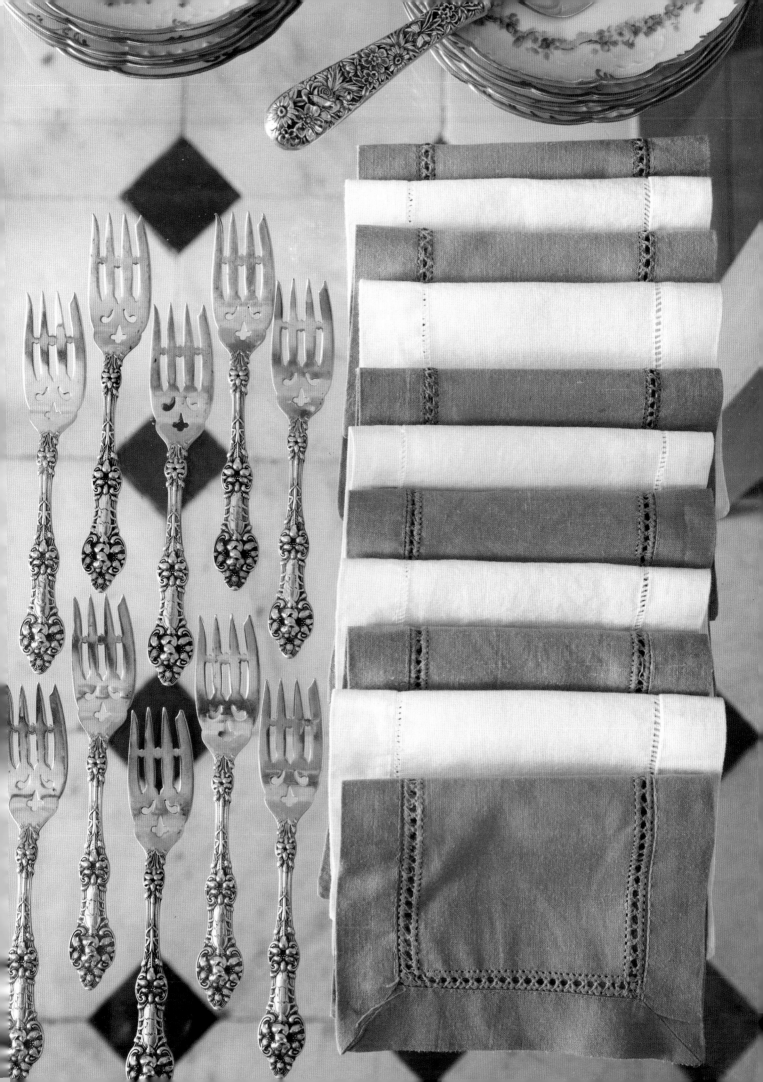

Contemporary Loft Dinner

Anyone who has lived in New York City has stories of neighbors. Those of us in apartment buildings find we generally have three kinds of neighbors— the ones with whom we exchange a polite hello but rarely any further conversation; the ones we wish would move; and the ones with whom we connect and whom we genuinely enjoy. During the ten years that Debra and I lived in Tribeca, a neighbor who fell into the last category was Jane Pratt of *Sassy* magazine, *Jane* magazine, and now of the website xoJane. One day in the elevator, Jane mentioned that she was planning a dinner party for ten of her friends, including Courtney Love, Michael Stipe, and Chris Martin. She told me she had booked the caterer and invited the guests, but could use my help with the look of the party. Of course, I agreed to lend a hand.

Jane lives in a beautifully decorated modern loft, but my favorite thing about the space is its sweeping view of the Hudson River. She agreed to let me rearrange her furniture for the party so that the dining table would be in front of the windows facing the river, providing a dramatic, constantly changing backdrop for the evening.

Jane's dining table wasn't large enough to seat ten comfortably, so I brought in a table made from a slab of unfinished mango wood and paired it with original Cherner chairs from the early 1960s. I decided that the tabletop design should play to the organic nature of the mango table, as well as the loft's modern sensibility. Italian glassware from the 1970s, blackened stainless-steel flatware, and napkins with a graphic pattern kept the volley between the two styles in play. Hand-thrown black pottery plates with an ochre center and an irregular asymmetrical shape were both organic and modern. For unusual place cards, I wrote guests' names with a chalk pen on amuse-bouche plates made by the same potter.

Finally, the table needed dynamic flowers. I chose Peruvian poppies in vibrant orange, apricot, and yellow. With their lively colors, tissue-thin petals, and intricate centers, these were stand-alone flowers, needing only to be placed at varying heights in simple test-tube-like clear glass vases. The sculptural stems twisting and turning the heads of the flowers added a playfulness to the design, and as the sun went down over the Hudson River, the poppies echoed the glorious tones of the sunset.

OPPOSITE: Clear vases of bright poppies placed at random around the sculptural candle holder gave a light feeling to the center of the table and worked well to balance the dark plates and flatware.

Never underestimate
the complexity
of a gorgeous, fully
opened poppy.

PREVIOUS PAGE, LEFT: Orange and yellow fruits, including persimmons, kumquats,
Buddha's hands, clementines, dragon fruits, lychee fruits, and cherries, were
piled onto modern compotes to add color at one end of the table. PREVIOUS
PAGE, RIGHT: The strong colors and curved stems of the poppies complemented
the loft's contemporary paintings. FOLLOWING PAGE: Low modern faux concrete
planters filled with ryegrass and succulents drew attention to the windows
without obstructing the magnificent Hudson River view.

PART II

By Day

In the Garden • An Old-Fashioned Ladies' Lunch
• Bold Bridal Shower • Bohemian Alfresco
• Vintage Road Trip

In the Garden

When four long-time friends who are avid gardeners came together for a late-spring luncheon, the hostess's garden was the natural choice for the location. I placed the table under the shade of a tall maple tree in a spot where it would be framed be two large fern-filled urns. In this lovely natural setting, my design for the table was driven by flowers. I wanted the table's centerpiece to be a study of spring for these women who love flowers, so instead of designing the centerpiece by color, I selected all my favorite spring flowers, knowing that their colors and shapes would come together in harmony. In a pale gray French wire basket chosen for its light, feminine look, I included anemones, Muscari, viburnum, ranunculus, nerines, parrot tulips, and hyacinths. With flowers ranging in tone from hot pink and pale lavender to vivid green and yellow, this centerpiece was spring distilled.

In honor of the occasion, which was the recent retirement of one of the guests, the hostess and I agreed that the table should have a more formal look than one would usually expect for lunch outside, so it was set with china, silverware, and white linen napkins. The choice of tablecloth was easy. A cloth of white linen with green embroidery showed off the flowers, and the crisp white linen looked fresh against the grass and surrounding greenery.

An important thing I've learned in my years of decorating for parties is that the right chairs can add another layer to the design. So, when I knew that I needed a strong accent of color to stand out against the lush green backdrop, I decided to incorporate it with chairs. I had rattan chairs that were in a style that looked perfectly at home in the garden setting painted bright neon pink. Against the white tablecloth and the verdant green setting, the chairs added just the right pop of color. Finally, a vintage copy of Vita Sackville-West's charming 1930s gardening book *Some Flowers* was tied with pink and green ribbon and placed on each chair.

OPPOSITE: The table's centerpiece was a profusion of spring flowers. This abundant bouquet of anemones, Muscari, viburnum, ranunculus, nerines, parrot tulips, and hyacinths was a bit oversized for the table, marking the luncheon as a special celebration. PRECEDING PAGE: Chinoiserie-style chairs painted neon pink punctuated the garden setting.

ABOVE LEFT: White cotton gauze protected the fully set table until guests arrived. ABOVE RIGHT: Each guest went home with a vintage gardening book. OPPOSITE: The center piece included flowers of many different textures, colors, and shapes. I make it a rule to use strongly scented flowers, such as hyacinths, only on a table located outside.

An Old-Fashioned Ladies' Lunch

When I was growing up in the South, my mother often hosted luncheons for small groups of friends. Whether the guests were a coterie from her study club, a few colleagues from the school where she taught, or members of her Sunday school class, I remember the luncheons as meals designed with careful attention to everything down to the smallest details. There were always perfectly ironed linens, formal china, silverware, my mother's collection of glassware designed by the great mid-century artist Dorothy Thorpe, and, of course, centerpieces of greenery or flowers, which most often came from our garden. I still recall a particularly beautiful arrangement that she made with bright pink and green caladium leaves in an ornate silver bowl. While at the time my favorite thing about my mother's luncheons may have been the leftover cheese straws and lemon meringue pie, today I realize what a strong impression her meticulously set tables made on me.

I had my mother in mind when designing the table for a luncheon given to celebrate the renewed friendships of six childhood friends who reconnected through Facebook, and I carefully handpicked items from the hostess's collections. She had an unusual assortment of children's silver napkin rings, which we used to hold reticella lace-bordered napkins. Her extensive collection of vintage painted china allowed us to use plates from a different pattern for each course, and her antique silverware complemented all of them. Exquisite hand-painted Italian glasses added another layer of beautiful detail. Finally, I asked the hostess to obtain a childhood photograph of each guest, and I put the photos in small silver frames to be used as place cards.

I decided to anchor the table's centerpiece with a spiral myrtle topiary planted in an heirloom silver basket. Miniature pink Phalaenopsis orchid plants in creamware coronets and Florentine cachepots were arranged around the topiary. Using blooming plants instead of cut flowers added to the charm of the tabletop design, and after the luncheon, each guest was able to take an orchid plant home as a favor.

OPPOSITE: Hand-painted china, antique silverware, and reticella-lace bordered napkins were pretty details on the table. FOLLOWING PAGE, LEFT: Guests took home the miniature Phalaenopsis orchid plants after the luncheon. FOLLOWING PAGE, RIGHT: A luxurious striped blue silk cloth with a square white damask overlay covered the table.

PREVIOUS PAGE: Small framed pictures of the guests as children served as place cards. ABOVE: The napkins were in silver napkin rings from the 1920s and 1930s. OPPOSITE: Robin's-egg blue hand-painted china plates were used for dessert.

Bold Bridal Shower

The colors for decorating a bridal shower seem to fall into three categories—the bride's chosen palette for the wedding, the hue of the bridesmaids' dresses, or soft pastels. None of these three schemes is ever a mistake, but for this early spring bridal shower, I felt the traditional paradigm could stand to be shaken up a little. Black and white plus one bold color has proven to be a foolproof formula for many events that I've styled, and since the hostess for the shower lived in a Tribeca loft decorated in black and white, that was clearly the way to go. Red, hot pink, and orange would all have worked well as the accent color, but when I thought about the time of year—spring—and the flowers available, the choice was obvious: it had to be yellow.

Choosing flowers was easy. Yellow is one of the first colors of spring when daffodils, forsythia, and ranunculus start to bloom. Another one of my favorite spring flowers is mimosa, which is available for only a short period of time. With its delicate fragrance and the bubble look of its blossoms, it reminds me of Champagne. I included yellow mini calla lilies because of their simple architectural lines. Then, several large arrangements of bright chromium yellow oncidium orchids added drama.

Bridal showers typically revolve around refreshments and opening presents. With that in mind, special attention should be given to the food presentation and the gift display. For this shower, I covered the buffet table in a sheet of black Lucite for a clean and modern look, and I decorated the table with not one, but five flower arrangements, each composed of a single type of yellow flower. White ceramic platters, clear Lucite stands, Lucite compotes, and even a Lucite platform to hold cheese beautifully displayed the food while maintaining a sharp, chic silhouette. I made sure to incorporate yellow food into the buffet. Cupcakes with yellow frosting

OPPOSITE: Gifts wrapped in black, white, and yellow reinforced the color scheme. FOLLOWING PAGE: Using only one type of flower in each arrangement gave a modern edge to the buffet design.

At every opportunity, we repeated the black, white, and yellow color scheme, even choosing black-and-white cookies and chocolate truffles wrapped in black foil.

Vanilla and chocolate cupcakes, both topped with yellow buttercream flowers, alternated on a tiered Lucite stand.

roses, yellow bell peppers, yellow cherry tomatoes, pineapple, and a bowl of lemons studded with stephanotis reinforced the yellow accent.

Many times I find a gift table to be problematic. While there is a practical need for a gift table—the presents have to go somewhere before they are opened—too often it ends up looking like a jumbled pile of wrapped boxes and gift bags. For this shower, I suggested we make the gift display a strong decorative element in and of itself. I asked the hostess to request that gifts be wrapped in black, white, and yellow. On the day of the party, we cleared off her bookshelves and placed small arrangements of yellow flowers here and there, and as guests arrived their gifts were placed on the shelves to great effect. It was one of my favorite elements of the room.

Playing up the bold, simple color scheme, small round tables were decorated with graphic black-and-white patterned tablecloths and mixed bouquets of yellow roses, ranunculus, daffodils, poppies, and Craspedia. As finishing touches, we brought in yellow lacquer serving trays and black-and-white patterned accent pillows.

ABOVE: Stephanotis blossoms were tucked into a pyramid of lemons.
OPPOSITE: Yellow flowers and lemons on the buffet contrasted beautifully
with black vases and the glossy black surface of the table. FOLLOWING
PAGE, LEFT: Bouquets of yellow flowers in black and white glass vases went
onto small round tables. FOLLOWING PAGE, RIGHT: I used several different
black and white patterns for the tablecloths, and black and white Eames
chairs surrounded the tables.

PRECEDING PAGE: Chromium yellow flowers and trays accented the black and white furniture. ABOVE: Even the dogs, Pearl and Lulu, fit the color scheme. OPPOSITE: A Murano glass vase held mimosa and orchids.

Bohemian Alfresco

"I'm having a *Meet the Fockers* luncheon" was the explanation my client gave for a small gathering that was giving her no small amount of anxiety. Her son had just become engaged, and he and his fiancée were bringing her parents to meet his parents for the first time. They planned a late afternoon lunch at my client's country house in the Hudson Valley, so she asked me to craft an environment that was warm and inviting. Because she is a venerable New York City hostess known for her creative parties with interesting themes and notable guests, I knew that it was important for the decor to have impact and a certain élan. After several conversations, we settled on an al fresco lunch in a colorful Bohemian style.

A successful Bohemian look relies on mixing colors and patterns in a way that is interesting and pleasing to the eye, but when creating this look, it is important not to mix too many different elements or the table may appear jumbled rather than chic. To enjoy the varied elements, you need to rest the eye with a few similar or matching components. For example, you might use only one type of chair, or a single type of flower.

With that caveat in mind, I started with a picnic table that had been stained a rich cerulean blue and surrounded the table with metal bistro chairs. Cushion covers and chair-back covers made from terra-cotta and ivory-striped canvas introduced a bold graphic element, and ceramic soup bowls added more patterns, as did playful mango and pink napkins of several different designs. For more layers of color, I used celadon and coral ceramic plates, red-handled flatware, and glasses in a mix of magenta, apple green, orange, and teal.

Simple flowers, many purchased from the local farmers market, were chosen for their lively colors. Dahlias, cosmos, sunflowers, clematis, jasmine, and zinnias were arranged in vibrant cobalt-blue and teal glass vases in an unstructured, carefree style. Large blue-painted iron lanterns were put out in case the late luncheon extended into the evening. The stage was set for a convivial afternoon of conversation and getting to know the soon-to-be in-laws.

OPPOSITE: The casual Bohemian style of the table was well suited to the patio setting. FOLLOWING PAGE: An overhead view shows the unusual blue stain on the table and the bold striped canvas chair-back covers and cushions. Dried artichokes held the napkins in place.

With bright flowers, casual ceramic dishes, bowls of cold soup, and colored glasses, the table epitomized summer dining.

Vintage Road Trip

An unusual round Victorian picnic basket that I found at an antique store and a classic car glimpsed as I drove past a gas station inspired an anniversary celebration last fall. Ten years earlier we'd designed the decor for a couple's New York City wedding, and the groom, now the father of two, came to me for help celebrating this significant occasion. He wanted to do something more unconventional than the usual dinner out. Remembering the picnic basket and thinking about the romance often associated with classic cars, I suggested a vintage road trip. He enthusiastically approved that idea and asked me to help him pull it off.

First, we talked about the location. My client is a filmmaker, and he remembered a scenic spot a location scout had shown him. This site, which was about an hour and a half outside of New York City and overlooked the Hudson River, seemed like the perfect destination for a road trip, and I knew just the right car. I rented a gorgeous cream-toned 1947 Mercury convertible from a classic car club, and we packed the trunk for a romantic retro-style picnic.

When I planned the picnic, practicality was, of course, a consideration, but I also wanted to create a beautiful ambience. I supplied several wool stadium blankets to layer on the ground for seating, as well as two Turkish floor pillows. The picnic lunch, which was provided by the couple's housekeeper, was packed into a traditional suitcase-style English picnic basket and a round Victorian wicker basket. Soup went into a pair of 1950s Coleman thermoses in their original plaid tote. For some bright fall color, I added fuchsia, orange, and green glasses for drinking and for soup, and colorful stopper bottles held water.

For me, no celebration, not even a picnic, is complete without flowers. A bouquet of ranunculus, scabiosa, anemones, cosmos, zinnias, fiddlehead ferns, and the last of the season's hydrangea was wrapped in tissue paper and placed on the car's back seat as a finishing touch for this sweetly sentimental celebration.

OPPOSITE: Even the packed trunk of this great 1947 Mercury convertible was stylish.

ABOVE: A Victorian basket held colorful glasses and bottles of water. Rolled napkins separated the glasses. OPPOSITE: A bouquet of country flowers fit the occasion. FOLLOWING PAGE: The Hudson River was the stunning backdrop for this autumn picnic.

PART III

Occasions

Moroccan Dinner • At Home for Rosh Hashanah
• A Venetian Birthday • Rustic Wedding

Moroccan Dinner

Travel always influences my creative perspective. Back in 2005, Debra and I visited Morocco, and of course I fell in love with all the vivid colors in the market stalls stacked with rugs, the vibrantly painted plaster walls of shops and riads, and the iconic tile work. Marrakesh is a beautiful city, and I wasn't surprised by the riot of color everwhere, but what captivated me more than anything were the decorative shapes, textures, and motifs woven throughout Moroccan design.

Last summer when Debra and I started planning a dinner party for fourteen at our house in the Hudson Valley, we thought about using our dining room, but that seemed too formal for the occasion. We thought about a dinner on the porch, but that seemed too casual. We were looking for something in between, something unexpected, when we hit upon the idea of having dinner in our 1906 stone carriage house. This structure has so many of the things we look for when searching for an event space for our clients: a large open area, a high ceiling, and a blank canvas to decorate. On top of this, the carriage house has gorgeous parchment-colored plaster walls, and the stone facade keeps it cool even on warm summer nights.

The decor direction was determined by Debra's choice of a Moroccan menu, and I was intrigued by the idea of designing a Moroccan setting without using color. My aim was to employ white to put the focus on the shapes and motifs I remembered so well from our trip.

For a strong visual element with thematic impact, we hung a collection of white Moroccan lanterns in the center of the carriage house, and we placed a long table directly beneath the lanterns. We covered the table with a fitted white linen cloth, and for seating we used whitewashed picnic benches with cushions covered in white

PRECEDING PAGE: A ceiling hung with Moroccan lanterns and a table glowing with candlelight welcomed guests to the carriage house. OPPOSITE: A tall arrangement of dried Bismarckia leaves and candles and lanterns added atmosphere to a corner of the carriage house. FOLLOWING PAGE, LEFT: Flat silver-bordered chargers purchased in Marrakesh and white glazed pottery plates carried through the white Moroccan tabletop design. FOLLOWING PAGE, RIGHT: Dark wood folding Syrian chairs with pearl inlay stood at either end of the table.

ABOVE: Guests' names were printed on strips of clear acetate and tied around the napkins with silver cord. OPPOSITE: Several traditional Moroccan rose water sprinklers were on the table.

To fill the space of the large carriage house, I created a vignette with a mixture of vintage and Moroccan items.

goatskin. A dark wood Syrian chair with pearl inlay was placed at each end of the table.

Flowers for the table were chosen for their distinctive shapes and for their pure white quality. Calla lilies, Phalaenopsis orchids, and cattleya orchids were placed in slender vases of several different heights. Large white king proteas added an exotic look to the table and were a powerful counterpoint to delicate clematis blossoms below. I wanted to avoid the wedding look that mixed bouquets of white flowers can give to a table, so I used only a few stems of a single type of flower in each vase.

I was also inspired by the restaurants in Marrakesh that are tucked away down dark alleys illuminated only by foot lanterns at night, so to guide our guests into dinner I lined the path to the carriage house with large white iron lanterns. As the sun was going down, our guests finished their cocktails on the porch and walked along the candlelit path to the carriage house. Inside, it was aglow with candles and old-fashioned oil lamps. Those plaster walls had never looked as beautiful as they did when bathed in that soft amber dancing light. As we closed the carriage house doors and sat down to a North African feast, I think we all felt transported far away.

OPPOSITE: A large incense burner, tall tapers in a tarnished silver candelabra, and glass vases holding vines of clematis blossoms were also on the table. Nearby were stacks of Moroccan floor pillows, a silver leather pouf, and a pair of metal garden chairs draped with a Moroccan wedding blanket. Black calla lilies in test tubes were hung on the back wall. FOLLOWING PAGE, LEFT: Clematis blossoms were in heavy glass Rosenthal vases. FOLLOWING PAGE, RIGHT: The flowers for the table were chosen for their tones of pure white and creamy ivory.

At Home for Rosh Hashanah

Some of the most meaningful celebrations are centered on religious holidays. These are moments when family and friends often gather for special meals. And traditions passed down through generations frequently enrich the experience of religious holidays, inviting each guest to remember earlier celebrations as they honor the occasion. Such was the case when a favorite longtime client called and asked me to help her with her annual Rosh Hashanah dinner. She wanted the table to have a smart, somewhat rustic style, and it was important to her that we include items that are traditional to her family's celebration of this holiday. She reminded me that she loves the color blue and that she loves flowers in dark, rich tones, and then she left the design of the tabletop up to me.

I covered a sixteen-foot table with a tailored cloth of slate-blue burlap, and I used the client's collection of hand-thrown pottery vases to hold the flowers. Deep red and burgundy dahlias, aubergine calla lilies, plum-toned Queen Anne's lace, nigella pods, black ornamental grasses, geranium leaves, and green cymbidium orchids went into vases of different shapes and sizes for a look that was autumnal without using the bright red, orange, and yellow tones that are more typically associated with fall. Taking a cue from the colors of the flowers, I used burgundy linen napkins in putty-colored ceramic napkin rings.

As is traditional, the hostess wanted apples and honey on the table to augur sweetness for the year ahead, so I loosely wove a basket out of manzanita branches and filled it with red apples. Small glass pots of honey placed along the length of the table looked particularly pretty in the diffused light of frosted blue and gray votive candles. Loose pomegranates arranged among the vases of flowers symbolized prosperity and renewal. Finally, a silver kiddush fountain—a special family treasure—was placed at one end of the table, and a challah in the round shape customary for Rosh Hashanah rested on a wooden board near the place setting for my client's father. Ready for guests, the table was sumptuous and full of meaningful symbolism, but not overly fancy—an inviting setting for a family celebrating the Jewish New Year.

OPPOSITE: A silver wine fountain with cups took pride of place on the table. FOLLOWING PAGE: The lights were lowered and the candles were lit just before guests were invited into the dining room.

Different varieties
of seasonal burgundy
dahlias were handsome
in earthenware vases.

ABOVE LEFT: A traditional round challah and a silver kiddush cup were on the table. ABOVE RIGHT: Place cards were held by small brass animals. OPPOSITE: Deep burgundy scabiosa and dahlias, aubergine calla lilies, reddish-brown millet, and burgundy Dutch Queen Anne's lace, all components of the centerpieces, are shown here individually. FOLLOWING PAGE: Apples and honey were on the table to bring sweetness in the year ahead. PAGES 122-123: Taper candles and votive candles added warmth to the deep windowsill and were styled next to the client's sculpture of carved phone books.

A Venetian Birthday

Very much alive-and-kicking is the best way to describe an older couple who have been clients of mine for many years. Splitting their time between New York City and Venice, this couple lives a life of marked contrasts—basking in the rich history and traditions of Venice and experiencing the vibrancy and energy unique to New York. When they contacted me to plan an intimate dinner party in New York City to celebrate both of them turning eighty years old, I knew we had to give equal attention to their two favorite locales. I suggested a Venetian-inspired dinner on their rooftop terrace in SoHo, and they both agreed that the idea was just right.

The dinner was planned for early fall in New York, a wonderful time of year when the weather would still be mild enough to allow dinner outside. I picked a spot for the dinner table right under a small pergola to give a cozy feeling amid the vast open sky and surrounding tall buildings. When I thought about Venice, two colors—gold and deep red—came to mind quickly, so I chose those to drive the look. As two birthdays were being celebrated, I suggested, well, actually insisted, that a pair of birthday cakes be featured as a part of the centerpiece of the table. One of their favorite bakeries in New York is Francois Payard, so we ordered two of the patisserie's signature chocolate cakes, which were decorated with gold embellishments. Taking a cue from the colors of those gorgeous brown and gold cakes, we used a dark brown bengaline tablecloth topped with a gold damask runner. For seating, we had the same brown bengaline fabric quilted and sewn into chair covers.

OPPOSITE: Each place setting was layered with details—a glass and gold Italian charger under a gold-banded plate, a place card with the guest's initials tied onto a brown-bordered gold linen napkin, and a Venetian mask with gold leaf applied. FOLLOWING PAGE, LEFT: Nothing is more romantic than head-to-head red roses in candlelight. FOLLOWING PAGE, RIGHT: Red and gold ribbon poles gave a festive Renaissance air to the scene.

Gold pillar candles nestle in red rose petals, offering a classically romantic look.

For this table, I never really considered using any flower other than red roses. It might seem trite, or banal, or even corny, but there is nothing like beautiful red roses to give a lush romantic look to a tabletop. Here I decided to use two red rose varieties, Cherry Love and Black Magic, which vary slightly in tone but complement each other. Because I wanted low, compact bouquets, I used seven dozen roses on this eight-foot-long table. I purchased the flowers three days before the party and immediately put them in warm water to allow the blossoms to open fully. Arrangements of these roses were placed down the length of the table, along with modern hurricane candleholders with gold pillar candles that filled the table with color and light.

The table was beautiful and elegant, but I wanted another reminder of Venice. My clients had a dozen Venetian masks in classic shapes but without any of the typical extravagant decorations. I added gold leaf to the masks, fully covering some masks and adding just splashes of gold to others, and I put a mask at each place setting as a party favor. With the candlelight reflecting off them, the gold-leaf masks were a particularly lovely addition to the table.

On the night of the party, the table was set, and from the terrace guests could take in the magical views of downtown Manhattan. There was the feeling of a room in the sky—and maybe, for a moment, the Grand Canal below.

FOLLOWING PAGE: Gold-embellished chocolate cakes were displayed on Venetian-glass cake stands.

LEFT: Venetian masks needed only touches of gold leaf to fit into the tabletop design.
ABOVE: Amethyst, ruby, aquamarine, emerald, amber, and cobalt flutes added a bit more color to the table and reminded me of Carnival.

Rustic Wedding

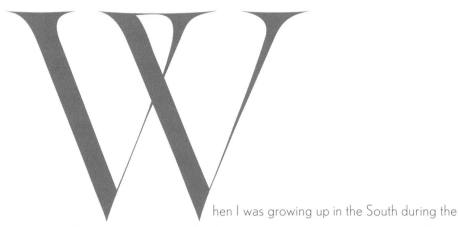

When I was growing up in the South during the 1960s and 1970s, two words that I would never have expected to hear used together were *rustic* and *wedding*. Weddings, unless they were very small, were formal dress-up affairs where Emily Post etiquette ruled the day. Happily for today's brides and grooms, that has changed. Over the last twenty years I have decorated weddings that have ranged from a white tie formal event to a barbecue in a field and everything in between, and I particularly like mixing elements that are formal and traditional with more relaxed elements so that the wedding decor reflects different aspects of the couple's personalities.

A Connecticut bride and groom contacted me after they had chosen for their wedding celebration one of the most beautiful bucolic settings in America: Blue Hill at Stone Barns in Pocantico Hills, New York. The ceremony was to be held in a chapel in Greenwich, Connecticut, and then guests would travel to Stone Barns for cocktails, dinner, and dancing.

Taking a cue from the textured stone walls of the HayLoft, I had tablecloths made from loden-green wide-weave cotton fabric that reminded me of burlap, and I dressed up this unconventional fabric choice with long runners of charcoal-toned metallic linen. Folded white linen napkins holding the dinner menus were placed directly on the tablecloth instead of on chargers or place plates for a less formal look. The wedding was in the fall, so I used autumnal components, including pears, moss, berries, and lichen, along with the gorgeous white flowers the bride had requested. Mercury-glass vases, silver cups and compotes, and clear glass containers were filled with roses, lilies, lisianthus, peonies, orchids, and parrot tulips and arranged on long tables. Magnolia leaves, iron cross begonia foliage, echeveria, and globe scabiosa gave an organic feeling to the floral compositions. The long stems of Phalaenopsis orchids arced gracefully over the low bouquets, and ivory pillar candles in distressed mercury glass photophores and in tall glass holders cast soft light on the tables.

The end result was a flawless balance of traditional and earthy the bride and groom had wanted, and the perfect way to launch their new life together.

OPPOSITE: This view of the table shows that all of the centerpiece components are anchored on the fourteen-inch-wide runner of charcoal-toned metallic linen.

Tall glass candleholders serve as modern-day candelabras, providing light without formality.

PREVIOUS PAGE: An abundance of flowers, greenery, fruit, and candles gave the table a full, generous aspect. FOLLOWING PAGE, LEFT: The menus were tucked into the folds of the triple-hemstitched white linen napkins. FOLLOWING PAGE, RIGHT: A few blossoms of white peonies, lilies, and parrot tulips filled a mercury-glass cup.

LYN AND STEVE

THIS MORNING'S FARM EGG
winter vegetables and greenhouse green

Hirsch Grüner Veltliner 'Heiligenstein' Kamptal, Austria 2011

MAINE LOBSTER
potato and shellfish chowd

Luli Chardonnay Santa Lucia High

ABOVE: As reminders of autumn, pears in distressed mercury-glass compotes appeared on all of the tables. OPPOSITE: We covered the bar with a slipcover of quilted silver metallic linen. An arrangement of magnolia leaves, camellia leaves, and cedar branches adorned the bar.

Thanksgiving with Heirlooms

Last fall, Gloria Vanderbilt, a dear client, emailed to say that she was hosting Thanksgiving dinner for friends and family. The holiday meal was to be at the home of her son Anderson Cooper, who lives in a converted firehouse in Manhattan's West Village. Gloria wanted to use one long table to seat twenty-four guests, and she asked me to design the tabletop.

When my clients entertain at home, I encourage them to use some of their own china, glassware, linens, and silverware instead of renting everything, because I feel that this gives a very personal touch to the table. I asked Gloria if she had any of her own things we could use, and she said she had a lot of her grandmother's china that had been made for the Breakers, the legendary summer "cottage" of her paternal grandparents, Alice and Cornelius Vanderbilt II. Vanderbilt family china, crystal, and silver, as well as Gloria's own collection of linens, was laid out in her dining room for me to consider. I thoroughly enjoyed selecting plates, crystal glassware, silver flatware, and silver serving pieces from her extraordinary collection. In addition to the antique items, Gloria made available her numerous chunks of rock crystal, carved glass votive candle holders, and silver animal figurines. I curated a tabletop of items from three generations in order to weave them into a design that would be unique for this occasion.

To start, instead of using one large tablecloth, I layered five white linen cloths, some trimmed with lace, some edged with crocheted trim, and others with double and triple hemstitching and embroidery. To these I added three different styles of white linen napkins, all with different types of trim—crochet, lace, and hemstitching.

Cut-crystal bud vases and rose bowls, all with the Cornelius Vanderbilt logo emblazoned in gold leaf, were among the items that I chose. The bud vases were used on guests' breakfast trays at the Breakers and Gloria told me that they were typically filled with red and purple anemones. I loved that bit of family history, and

OPPOSITE: A small vignette of flowers and family silver adorned a table just outside the dining area. PRECEDING PAGE: For the center of the table, red and purple flowers went into a large silver bowl from Gloria Vanderbilt's family collection.

The table had so many interesting components that each place setting told its own story.

let it guide my flower choices for the table. A large arrangement of purple lisianthus, deep-red amaryllis, bordeaux-toned roses, red parrot tulips, and red and purple anemones went into a massive silver footed bowl in the center of the twenty-two-foot table. Down the length of the table I placed the rose bowls from the Breakers, which were filled with red roses, and the cut-crystal bud vases, which held anemones. Among the arrangements of flowers, I placed chunks of clear rock crystal, several silver fish, three dozen carved glass votive candles, and two magnificent silver peacocks. The combination of objects and tableware with origins ranging from the Gilded Age to the twenty-first century melded together for a look that was both intriguing and elegant.

When I went to the converted firehouse for a site visit, the interior, which reminded me of an English gentlemen's club, made me feel like I was in a Noel Coward play, so I told Gloria that I thought the background music for this dinner should be songs from the soundtracks of Woody Allen movies. She agreed and also introduced me to the British dance-band era music of another favorite musician of hers, Ray Noble. I compiled a playlist by weaving together scores from *Bullets Over Broadway*, *Manhattan*, *Radio Days*, and *Midnight in Paris* with the greatest hits from the Ray Noble Orchestra.

Shortly after the dinner concluded and all the guests were gone, I received an email from Gloria. It was brief and to the point. It read, "Thank you, DeJuan. The evening was perfect. How often in a lifetime can one say that?"

FOLLOWING PAGE: Crystal vases and decanters were originally used at the Breakers.

ABOVE LEFT: Vintage lace-trimmed napkins added to the heirloom design of the table. ABOVE RIGHT: Silver fish were carefully placed so that they appeared to be swimming among the objects on the table. OPPOSITE: An impressive fourteen-inch tall, English silver peacock struts the length of the table.

Holiday Buffet

O

ne of my favorite memories of growing up in Alabama is attending the wedding of the governor's daughter. Following the wedding, a reception was held at the Governor's Mansion in Montgomery. There was an enormous pink-and-white-striped tent on the lawn, an orchestra playing, waiters circulating with canapés, fountains of sparkling wine, and more tables of food than I had ever seen. Going from buffet to buffet, I saw lavish displays of Gulf Coast seafood, men in white jackets carving roast turkeys and huge slabs of roast beef, and tray after tray of tea sandwiches, cheese straws, and deviled eggs. The desserts served went way beyond the wedding cake, and there were tables of classic Southern cakes, petits fours by the thousands, and gallons of punch. As a teenager, I was, of course, impressed with the quantities of food, but I was also impressed with how beautifully the food was displayed. The tables were covered in pure white linen and swagged with smilax vines. Silver champagne buckets filled with camellias (the Alabama state flower) and Grecian-style urns with huge arrangements of white gladioli marked the buffets. Cakes were on tall cut-glass stands and ornate silver cake plateaus; silver serving trays were heavy with baroque embellishments; enormous garlanded silver pedestal bowls filled with ice contained mountains of shrimp; and punch was served from cut-crystal Fostoria punch bowls. These generous, artfully presented buffets stayed in my memory, and although styles have changed, I put the same kind of care used at that wedding into the buffets that I design for my clients and for my own entertaining.

When Debra and I invited several friends for a holiday supper a few weeks before Christmas, I had the idea of creating a buffet in the style of a Flemish still life. I cleared a spot in our library and placed the buffet table in front of a window and bookshelves for a backdrop that beautifully framed the table on two sides with books, a

OPPOSITE: In the tradition of a still life, this arrangement included many types of flowers and foliage. FOLLOWING PAGE: My rule of thumb for styling buffets is to have one large focal point and several additional points of interest other than food. Here, the flower arrangement was the focal point, and the candles and the items around the base of the arrangement were the points of interest.

Osage oranges, decumis fruits, and bundles of asparagus were chosen for their bright green color and their unusual textures.

classic still-life element. A large floral arrangement in the loose, tumbling style of seventeenth-century still lifes went onto one end of the buffet. Inspired by the colors of the striped silk draperies in the room and by the rich hues of the holiday season, I used flowers and foliage in tones of bordeaux, crimson, burgundy, gold, apricot, deep orange, and violet. Roses, dahlias, echeveria, parrot tulips, hanging amaranthus, begonia leaves, and ornamental kale were arranged in a tall vase with an antique-brass finish. Around the base of the vase, I mounded pomegranates and placed a silver trophy filled with black Concord grapes and a silver stand stacked with decumis fruits, Osage oranges, and bundles of asparagus.

I wanted the presentation of the food to be a part of the still life, so I chose silver trays, a hammered silver bowl, and a glass compote as serving pieces, and a sauce went into a painted china gravy boat. I especially liked the strong white accent that a ceramic soup tureen with a timeless shape lent to the scene. An antique silver ice bucket held silver flatware neatly rolled in hemstitched linen napkins. The light from four cathedral candles was just enough to illuminate the dark paneled shutters behind the table, and a draped tablecloth of celery-green faille was the perfect foil for this studied composition. The final tableau was just as I had hoped.

Instead of a large arrangement of flowers, an arrangement of greenery with just a few flowers works well on a buffet. This one included umbrella fern, variegated aucuba, eucalyptus, ivy berries, variegated ivy, dill blossoms, yellow gloriosa lilies, Brunia, and viburnum.

Christmas in the Country

Debra and I celebrate Christmas with our family at our house in the Hudson Valley. While we have several Christmas traditions, such as wearing matching pajamas on Christmas morning, I like to vary the look of our holiday decorations from year to year. For maximum impact, I focus on a few key places to decorate—the mantels in the main rooms downstairs and the entrance hall that connects those rooms—and I think back over things that inspired me during the previous year as I plan our decorations.

A picture of some extraordinary Christmas ornaments made in Provence from dried lavender and velvet ribbons sparked the idea of incorporating decorative elements associated with southern France, such as lavender wands, lemons, pomegranates, and herbs, into this year's entrance hall decorations. I tied full garlands made of cedar, fir, and rosemary to the banister of the entrance hall staircase with wide terra-cotta-colored velvet ribbon. A garland of lemons and bunched salal leaves was laid on top of the greenery in alternating swags. Using two garlands gave a generous look to the banister, and the abundance of cedar, fir, rosemary, and lemons filled the air with a wonderful fragrance. I coiled the ends of the garlands around the newel-post and placed willow baskets full of classic Provençal elements—pomegranates, lemons, dried lavender, and lavender wands nested in hay—at the base. I also included a basket of cinnamon sticks for their scent.

To complement the South of France–style components in the entrance hall, I added a holiday topiary. I purchased a cut Douglas fir, and I trimmed the lower branches off the trunk and shaped the upper limbs into a classic topiary shape. I "planted" the tree in a terra-cotta planter filled with sand and topped with sheet moss, and styled pomegranates at the base of the trunk, which itself was festooned with oversized brown double-faced satin ribbon. As an added bonus, this topiary lasted longer than any of the other live decorations in the house, well into mid-January, even without being watered.

OPPOSITE: A Douglas fir with the lower branches removed became an unusual holiday topiary.

Baskets of dried
lavender, cinnamon
sticks, lemons,
and pomegranates
nicely balanced
the garlands
on the staircase.

FOLLOWING PAGE, LEFT: The willow baskets all had different shapes. FOLLOWING PAGE, RIGHT: Lavender, both in bundles and in wands, added its wonderful fragrance to the entrance hall.

I decorated the mantel in our front parlor as an homage to the Magi. The concept of this display took shape when I found three vintage-style crowns at a specialty design store in Manhattan a month or so before the holidays. I covered a three-tiered platform with gold-studded hunter green silk velvet and placed the crowns on the platform. Hefty cathedral candles stood on either side of the platform. A glass pedestal vase planted with Royal Velvet amaryllis was on each end of the mantel. As an effective addition to the mantel decor, I outlined the mirror above the mantel with wild smilax vines that I had sprayed here and there with gold paint. The gold paint caught the candlelight and gave an illuminated quality to the dark leaves.

The most prominent architectural feature in our back parlor is a bright white marble mantel fitted with a black iron coal grate insert—all original to the 1851 house. For this Christmas, I wanted to give the mantel a less traditional look, but I also wanted to harmonize with the bold black and white of the mantel and the unusual ebony-framed oval convex mirror that hangs over it, so I used Art Deco black glass vases filled with pearlized glass Christmas ornaments, round frosted crystal vases of black calla lilies, and black taper candles. Heavily flocked mountain laurel branches in tall black glass vases framed this composition. For detail, I tucked silver sleigh bells and black votive candles into the faux snow I'd sprinkled on the mantel. This fireplace no longer works, so I filled the coal grate with flocked pinecones and pearlized glass ornaments.

Our cozy library is smaller than the other rooms in the house. Because of the limited scale, I wanted to keep the decorations simple. A garland of mixed evergreens rested on the mantel shelf and trailed down to the floor on either side. Like the garland in the entrance hall, it gave off that wonderful evergreen scent. I found a box of vintage French Christmas cards at the Chelsea flea market, and I decided to repurpose them by cutting them into letters of the alphabet and adding them to the garland. The mantel is small, and so was my message: Peace on Earth. I scattered other letters up and down the sides of the garland and anchored the ends with two arrangements of red roses in mercury-glass vases. A pyramid of bright green apples nested in "manger hay" filled the opening of the fireplace.

Our final Christmas decoration is always the tree, which is long on sentiment and short on beauty—a very personal part of our holiday look. A day or so before Christmas, when our children and their spouses have arrived, we pull out battered boxes of ornaments that we have collected through the years, many of them made by the children in nursery school or later as art class projects, and we trim the tree with homely yet much-cherished ornaments. Then it feels like Christmas.

OPPOSITE: To make one garland, lemons and salal leaves were threaded onto grosgrain ribbon with heavy-gauge florist wire used as a needle. FOLLOWING PAGE, LEFT: Only a few of the smilax leaves were sprayed gold. FOLLOWING PAGE, RIGHT: Instead of laying a garland on the mantel, I framed the mirror with a garland of wild smilax.

ABOVE: Flocked pinecones make this scene look like Christmas with no need to disrupt the black-and-white scheme by introducing red or green. OPPOSITE: Black and white decorations gave the mantel a festive, wintry look and were beautiful against the purple walls. FOLLOWING PAGE, LEFT: Vintage French Christmas cards were cut into letters. FOLLOWING PAGE, RIGHT: The cut-out letters were tucked into the garland.

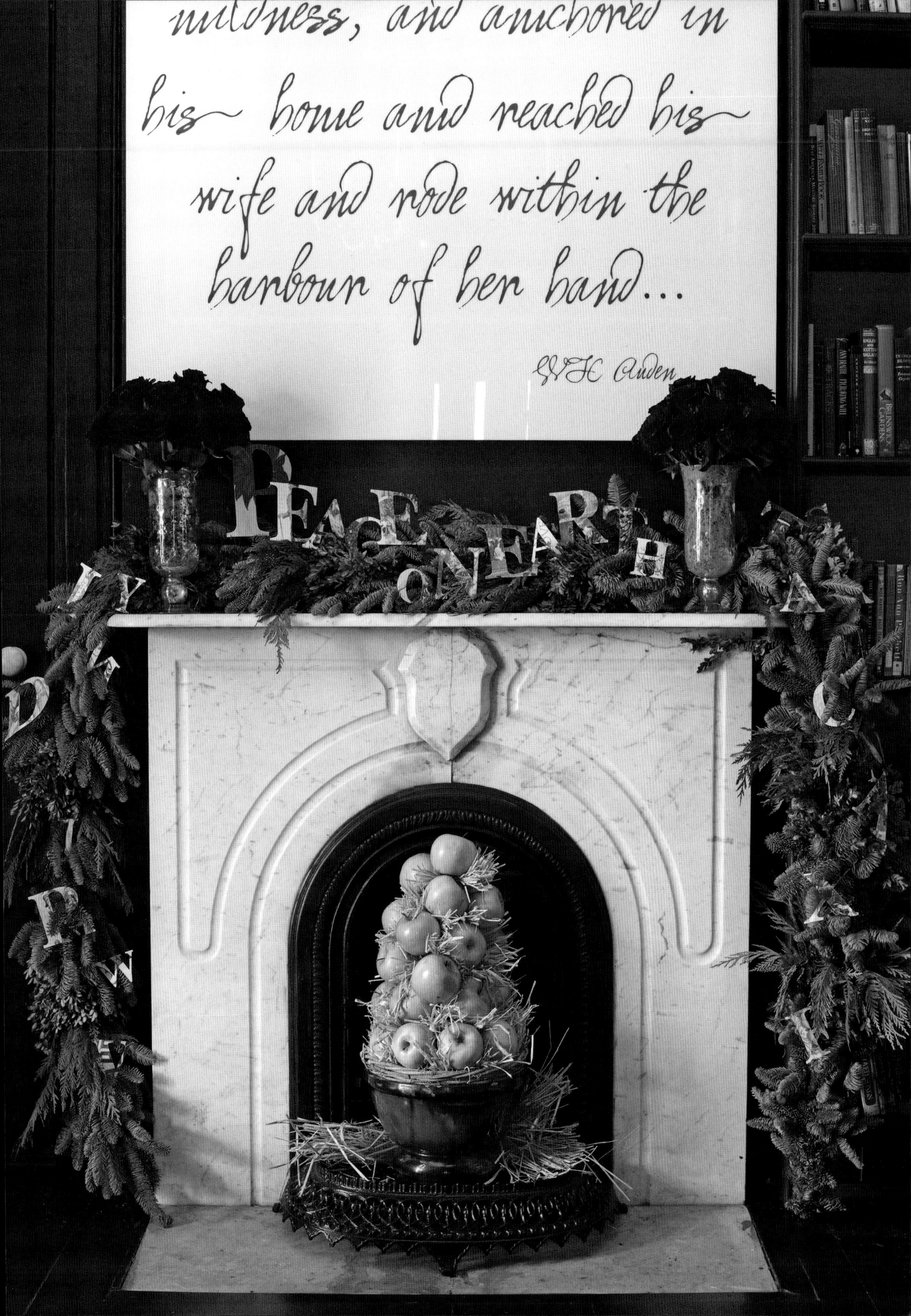
mildness, and anchored in
his home and reached his
wife and rode within the
harbour of her hand...
W.H. Auden
PEACE
ON EARTH

Dinner to Welcome the New Year

I have found that what most people—including myself—really want to do on New Year's Eve is celebrate. For several years, Debra and I have celebrated New Year's Eve with friends at Blackberry Farm in Tennessee. There, we enjoy an evening of great food, live music, and even a midnight balloon drop with a festive group of likeminded people, and it is the perfect way to usher in the new year. However, on the first January weekend that we're back in New York, I also like to celebrate the transition with an intimate dinner at home for family and a few friends, more quietly marking the holiday.

For one such dinner on a snowy night in early January, I set about planning a tranquil look. Taking the concept of quiet as my cue, I used a narrow palette of white, gray, and silver enhanced with crystal and candlelight, and I kept flowers to a minimum. With this limited range of colors, texture was important, even when it came to the tablecloth, so I layered two for extra impact: a neutral gray linen cloth covered the entire table, and an heirloom white damask cloth made a wide stripe across the table's center. Napkins of white Irish linen trimmed with pale gray and old-fashioned faggoting tied the two cloths together visually.

As a calm, reflective focal point, I created a dense oval ring of deer moss, eucalyptus berries, Brunia, and velvety dusty miller leaves. Candles floated in a shallow glass dish in the center of the ring. At each end of the table, an etched mercury-glass vase held stems of white amaryllis and hybrid Sumatra amaryllis. I felt that this beautiful, quiet table needed some sparkle, so I filled the center with candles. Two tall crystal candelabras, thin taper candles, pillar candles on chunky glass holders, and votive candles in textured mercury-glass holders added life. For ease of conversation at this intimate dinner, I needed there to be a clear sight line across the table, so other than the tall crystal candelabras, all the table components had a low profile. I even chose glasses with short stems to achieve this effect.

I wanted the design to be slightly sentimental, so I set the table with vintage family silverware, as a nod to the old, and with contemporary Limoges china, as a nod to the new. The conversation that evening followed that theme, as we shared our trials and triumphs of the previous year and considered our individual voyages going forward into the new one.

OPPOSITE: With its hushed tones, the table had an elegant serenity.

PRECEDING PAGE: Candles floating in the center made the ring of silver and gray-green deer moss, eucalyptus berries, Brunia, and dusty miller leaves seem to glow. ABOVE AND OPPOSITE: Dusty miller leaves gave a softness to the ring of greenery and to the small amaryllis bouquets.

PART V

Workbook

Flowers and Containers • Breakaway Bouquets
• Potted Plants • One Arrangement, Three Ways
• Diagrams • Caring for Flowers • Resources

In this lovely green and white composition, roses in shades of white are arranged in silver cups, and a silver vase holds green-and-white parrot tulips. Spheres of moss and a miniature cedar plant are styled among the flowers.

1
Flowers and Containers

Selecting the right vase is a fundamental part of creating a flower arrangement. While I don't go by any hard and fast rules for this, I choose combinations that are pleasing to the eye and that suit the overall tabletop or room design, and I always keep in mind that attention should fall first on the flowers, not on the container. Sometimes I closely match the style of the vase to the flowers, while other times I contrast the flowers and container. An elegant stem of Phalaenopsis orchids in a tall, slender glass vase is an easy choice, but I also like the contrast of humble farm-stand coxcombs in an antique Chinese export bowl. The first flowers that I sent to Debra, when we were sixteen, were daisies in a simple basket with a handle. Corny as that arrangement was, the daisies looked so pretty in the basket that the overall effect was charming.

For arranging flowers in my home, I have four different collections of vases—colored glass, silver, pottery and metal, and clear glass. These vases are shown on the following pages and used to illustrate some of my favorite pairings of flowers and containers, including earthy orange flowers in a pottery vase, ladylike muted lavender roses in a silver cup, bold red flowers in a clear glass vase with prunts, and cosmos from my garden in a teal glass vase.

OPPOSITE: Cobalt vases of jasmine and clematis vines and teal vases of cosmos and dahlias were paired with colored water and wineglasses and an orange elephant-shaped sauce boat to make this table a riot of color.

Colored Vases

My collection of colored glass vases includes blue and green Dansk vases from the 1960s, as well as a striped Murano-glass vase that my daughter Molly bought for me in Italy. Most of my colored vases are used to hold only a few stems of flowers, because I've found that when the vase isn't crowded with stems, light can pass through, illuminating the color for a pretty effect.

When using colored glass vases, I like either to use a vase that contrasts with the color of flowers—bright yellow tulips in a carnelian vase—or to marry the color of the flowers with a vase of the same hue, such as placing a few stems of viburnum in a moss-green tumbler.

THIS PAGE: Ocean Song roses with a collar of begonia leaves are complemented by a silver vase.
OPPOSITE: Amnesia roses, Ocean Song roses, Montha roses, and Quicksand roses, all in muted shades of lavender, combine for a romantic vintage look.

Silver Containers

Until about thirty years ago, silver vases, bowls, and epergnes were the definitive choices for formal floral arrangements. They were a logical standard for traditional floral design, because a bright silver surface is beautiful against almost any flower. A variety of silver containers is still a useful and elegant part of a vase collection for your home.

Currently, silver vases also come with mirrored surfaces, mercury-glass coatings, and metallic glazes, and the shapes of today's silver containers go way beyond the classic Revere bowls and mint julep cups of the past. These days there are trapezoidal and gourd-shaped vases, and those unusual shapes take on an even more glamorous look with a polished silver finish.

A collection of silver containers should include both old and new styles. While a bouquet of two dozen roses in an engraved silver wine cooler is timeless, a curvy mercury-glass gourd is just right to hold one or two stems of cymbidium orchids.

The boldness of orange in
many shades gave this small
bouquet a strong presence.

Metal and Pottery Vases

What I love about pottery and metal is their earthy quality and they way they add warmth to the design of a table centerpiece. I've collected pottery vases and metal containers for years, starting with a 1932 pewter fraternity mug that Debra gave me for my sixteenth birthday. I still use it to hold lily of the valley in the spring. Making purchases from fine art galleries, as well as tag sales, online auctions, and even farmers markets, has yielded a collection that I use throughout the year.

I seek out metal containers with an aged patina that gives them great character, and I try to find unusual pieces, such as the vintage test-tube clamp and stand that I bought at a flea market. While not originally intended to serve as a container for flowers, it makes them all look like specimen blooms.

I prefer pottery vases with earth-tone glazes, because they harmonize as well with an arrangement of exotic orchids as they do with a bouquet of thistle and wildflowers.

Tulips, ranunculus and amaryllis in closely matched shades of crimson seemed to fuse together for a powerful contrast to the chalk gray painting in the background.

Clear Glass Vases

Clear glass vases are a mainstay for flower arranging. Available in a wide range of sizes and shapes, they are the best containers for showing off flowers from stems to blossoms. I also like how they can be paired with other types of vases when creating a table centerpiece with several components.

The clear glass vases in my personal collection were chosen for their interesting shapes. They include a glass cornucopia that often holds big heads of hydrangea from my garden and Rosenthal spheres that are especially complementary to Casa Blanca lilies. Recently, I found a supply of chemist beakers and flasks at an antique fair and was drawn to the simplicity of their silhouettes; they have become my go-to vases when I arrange flowers for our home.

2
Breakaway
Bouquets

One of the sweetest techniques I have used over the years is to create a breakaway bouquet. Essentially, a breakaway bouquet consists of several small bouquets placed close together in one vase to create what appears to be a single large arrangement. At the end of the party, the arrangement can easily be disassembled and the small bouquets wrapped in tissue paper, tied with ribbon, and given to guests as they leave.

There are seven identical smaller bouquets in the breakaway arrangement shown here. The recipe for each bouquet is three roses, three anemones, two Italian dianthuses, six ranunculus, six stems of Viburnum Lucidum, and one small artichoke on its stem.

Each bouquet was tied with raffia, and all seven bouquets were placed in a twelve-inch bowl of water. Angling the bouquets in the bowl instead of standing them straight up helped to give the overall arrangement a pretty shape.

Individual bouquets were
wrapped in waxed tissue
paper and tied with ribbon
for guests to take home.

3

Potted Plants

Instead of arranging cut flowers in a vase, I sometimes repot small blooming plants into a cachepot, a china bowl, or an interesting container for a delightful effect. I find that plants with small-scale blossoms, such as tête-à-tête daffodils, cyclamen, miniature azaleas, and pansies are easiest to use and lend a charming look to the finished design. Here, three primrose plants were grouped in a silver pedestal bowl and sheet moss was tucked around the edges.

4

One Arrangement, Three Ways

For a long table, a centerpiece composed of several different elements instead of one long flower arrangement has a casual elegance. As shown here and on the following page, the centerpiece can have only a few components, or it can be a complex configuration of plants and flowers. The centerpiece pictured at top is a balanced symmetrical arrangement of mounds of Irish moss, myrtle topiaries, and a maidenhair fern plant. Using one type of container, silver in this case, gives a finished look. In the bottom picture, simple blossoms of ranunculus and anemones in clear glass vases were added to the centerpieces. This technique of using only a few blooms on a table is especially effective with flowers of exceptional texture, color, or size. Open roses, peonies, amaryllis, and camellias would also work well in this type of design.

Taking this design a step further, bouquets of roses, anemones, viburnum, ranunculus, and lilacs replaced the single blossoms, and fiddlehead ferns were added for their spiral shape. The use of all silver containers for the plants and the flowers, with the exception of one glass vase, gave a purposeful continuity to the centerpiece.

The method of creating a base arrangement, in this case using plants and candles, is a useful way of establishing a starting point to a centerpiece. Starting with a base arrangement ensures that you are covering enough space on the table, and then you have the freedom to keep it as is or add more elements to the composition. A variation on this centerpiece might start with a base of three arrangements of fruit, perhaps pyramids of pomegranates in silver bowls, and a dozen mercury-glass votive candles. Single blossoms of open burgundy peonies in small silver cups could come next, and small bouquets of deep red tea roses in mercury-glass tumblers could be added if you wanted to fill out the centerpiece even more. The beauty of this concept is that the variations are endless.

5

Centerpiece Mapping

It is important to me that every centerpiece I create is unique for the occasion at hand. That said, I do use some of the same vase and candle configurations over and over. While the flowers, vases, and candles themselves vary, their placement adheres to time-tested formulas.

Each of the five centerpiece blueprints shown here can be used to create a beautifully balanced tablescape. The maps are based on a rectangular table eight feet long and forty-two inches wide and a round table with a seventy-two-inch diameter.

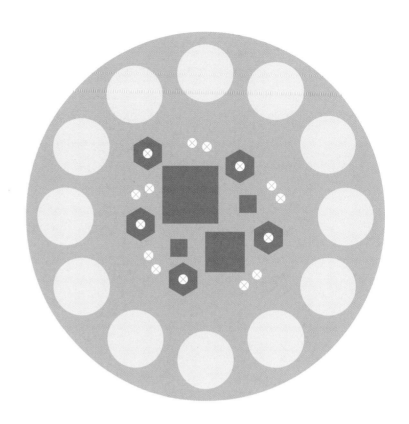

ABOVE: Four floral arrangements, one in a nine- to eleven-inch square vase, one in a six- to eight-inch square vase, and two in four-inch square vases are surrounded by five candlesticks with eighteen-inch tall tapers and ten votive candles.

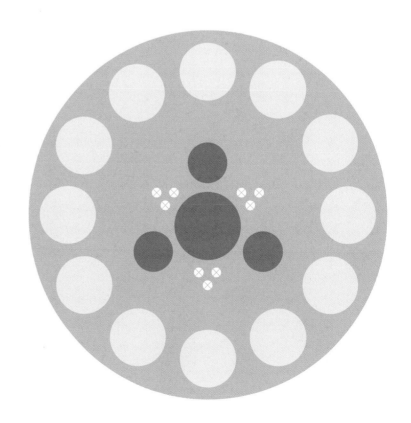

This centerpiece is composed of three floral arrangements, one in an eight- to ten-inch-diameter container and two in five- to seven-inch-diameter containers on either side of the first, and a dozen votive candles.

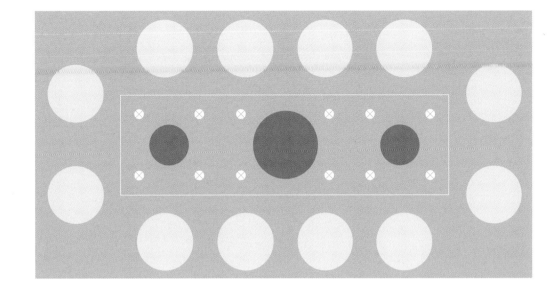

Four bouquets, each in a five- to seven-inch-diameter container, are arranged with sixteen votive candles.

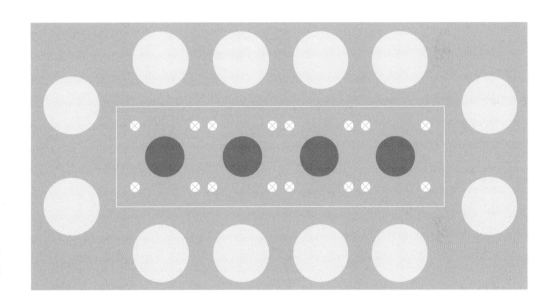

Four candlesticks holding eighteen-inch-tall tapers alternate with three bouquets in six- to seven-inch-diameter containers and are outlined with twelve votive candles.

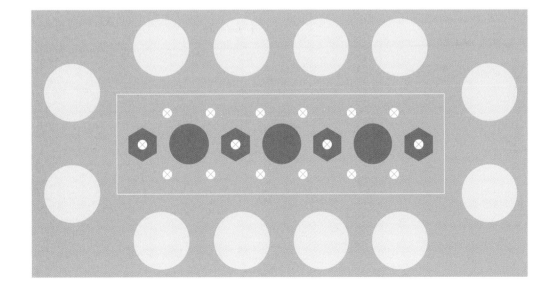

6

Caring for Flowers

Whether you are dealing with flowers from your garden or from a florist, a correct stem cut is necessary to ensure that they last. Soft- to semi-hard-stemmed flowers, such as roses, tulips, ranunculus, and anemones, should be cut with floral shears or a sharp knife. For the woody stems of hydrangeas, lilacs, and viburnum, use gardening shears. All cuts should be at an angle to increase the surface area of the stem so that the flowers can take in more water, and woody stems should be split vertically with shears after the angled cuts are made.

Once their stems have been properly cut, I recommend letting flowers drink for an hour or so before arranging them. Stand them straight up in a bucket of water and give them time to hydrate completely so that water goes all the way through the stems to the leaves and blossoms. The flowers will be firmer and easier to handle once they are full of water.

When you finish with a bouquet, check to ensure that the ends of all the stems are completely submerged in water. Sometimes stems are placed at a sharp angle to create a nice shape for the arrangement as a whole. After a day or so, as the flowers drink, the water level gets lower and the ends of the angled stems may end up above the waterline, which will quickly cause the flowers to wilt. Prevent this by adding water often.

To help your flowers last as long as possible, change the water every day or two, re-cutting the stems each time, and keep them in a cool place, out of direct sunlight, even in air-conditioned rooms.

Basic Flower
Arranging
Tools
and Supplies

WATER PICKS
Use these tubes to hold
flowers with short stems
when you want to include
them in an arrangement with
longer-stemmed flowers.

RAFFIA
This natural material is
perfect for tying
handheld bouquets. It
gets stronger when wet.

**SHALLOW GLASS
BOWLS**
These bowls can be used
as liners in deep containers
and they can be used to
hold floral foam when you
want to create a floral
arrangement on a flat
surface, like a pedestal.

FLORIST TAPE
Use either clear or green florist
tape to create a grid over a
container in order to hold
stems in place without using
floral foam. Also use for
securing floral foam in a vase.

WIRE CUTTERS
This tool is necessary for cutting most gauges of wire used in floral design.

SCISSORS
Always keep a pair of sharp scissors on hand for cutting tender stems and trimming leaves.

SHEARS
A pair of floral shears that cuts all types of stems is the most valuable tool for floral design.

FLORAL WIRE
Floral wire comes in varying gauges. Heavy-gauge wire is used for making evergreen garlands and wreaths. Lighter gauge wire is used for boutonnieres.

WIRED PICKS
These picks come in different lengths and are wrapped around soft stems as support.

FLORISTS' KNIVES
Use these knives to make angled cuts on stems. Keep the blades sharp.

Resources

CALLIGRAPHY

Deborah Delaney
212-877-8773

**CHAIR, TABLE, AND
TABLETOP RENTALS**

Party Rental Ltd.
201-727-4700
www.partyrentalltd.com

Something Different Party Rental
973-742-1779
www.sdpartyrental.com

**CHINA, GLASSWARE, AND
TABLETOP ACCESSORIES**

Anthropologie
800-309-2500
www.anthropologie.com

Bloomingdale's
800-777-0000
www.bloomingdales.com

Boutross Fine Linens
800-227-7781
www.boutross.com

CB2
800-606-6252
www.cb2.com

Global Table
212-431-5839
www.globaltable.com

Hive
561-514-0322
www.hivepalmbeach.com

Jered's Pottery
510-680-5444
www.jeredspottery.com

John Derian Company
800-677-3207
www.johnderian.com

La Maison Supreme
212-929-2615
www.lamaisonsupreme.com

Le Jacquard Français
www.le-jacquard-francais.com

Mary Mahoney
561-655-8288
www.marymahoney.com

Meg Cohen
212-966-3733
www.megcohendesign.com

Mizzonk
www.mizzonk.com

Papyrus
800-789-1649
www.papyrusonline.com

Restoration Hardware
800-762-1005
www.restorationhardware.com

Saks Fifth Avenue
877-551-7257
www.saksfifthavenue.com

T&T PlasticLand
212-925-6376
www.ttplasticland.com

Venice Buys
858-270-6769
stores.venicebuysmasks.com

Williams-Sonoma
877-812-6235
www.williams-sonoma.com

FLORAL SUPPLIES

B&J Florist Supply Company
212-564-6086

Jamali Floral and Garden Supplies
212-244-4025
www.jamaligarden.com

Mueller Brothers Florists
973-623-0171

FURNITURE AND PROPS

Bridge Furniture
& Props New York
718-916-9706
www.nybridgeprops.com

Patrick J. Tyner Skullduggery
Furnishings
www.skullduggeryfurnishings.com

HOME ACCESSORIES

ABC Carpet & Home
646-602-3101
www.abchome.com

Ballard Designs
800-536-7551
www.ballarddesigns.com

Billy Reid
877-757-3934
www.billyreid.com

John Derian Company
800-677-3207
www.johnderian.com

Jonathan Adler
800-963-0891
www.jonathanadler.com

Pottery Barn
888-779-5176
www.potterybarn.com

Schoolhouse Electric
& Supply Co.
800-630-7113
www.schoolhouseelectric.com

PLANTS

Foliage Garden
212-989-3089
www.foliagegarden.com

NY Topiary
646-380-6096
www.nytopiary.com

VASES

Accent Decor
800-385-5114
www.accentdecor.com

Antiques Barn at Water Street
Market
845-255-1403
www.newpaltzantiquesbarn.com

Jamali Floral and Garden Supplies
212-244-4025
www.jamaligarden.com

Jonathan Adler
800-963-0891
www.jonathanadler.com

Planter Resource
212-206-7687
www.planterresource.com

Rosenthal
800-596-3503
www.rosenthalusa-shop.com

When you bring beauty, care, and attention to the occasion, you mark the moment—for a lifetime.

Acknowledgments

Many, many, many thanks to:

The wonderful team at Rizzoli, especially Charles Miers and Kathleen Jayes, the most patient, encouraging editor a first-time author could hope to find.

My agent, Jill Cohen, whose unwavering enthusiasm was a constant source of encouragement.

The very talented Doug Turshen and his able partner David Huang for taking remarkable care with every single layout and for keeping my vision on track.

Monica Buck for taking one gorgeous photograph after another, and for always working tirelessly to get the perfect shot.

Charlotte Moss for all those gentle nudges. This book would not have happened without them.

Dorothea and Jon Bon Jovi for their support and friendship.

Anderson Cooper, Jane Pratt, Lisa and Richard Baker, Deborah and David Roberts, and Colleen Hess for their generosity in allowing us to photograph in their homes, and Gloria Vanderbilt for letting us photograph her family's Thanksgiving dinner.

Deirdre Featherstone for loaning her beautiful antiques. Patrick Tyner for his distinctive furniture finishes. Margaret and Jack Dabrusin for the use of their spectacular 1947 Mercury convertible.

My company's brilliant, uncompromising Senior Designer, Jay Bell, and talented Designer, Dora Boling. Our amazing production and support team: Nakisa Stroud, Angel Castillo, Ernesto Crisostomo, Welbin Bernavides, Biany Mora, Margo Ackerman, Pamela Taylor, Kimberly Borras, and Emma Ritcey.

My business partner Robert Stroud.

And most of all, my wife and business partner, Debra Stroud.

First published in the United States of America in 2016
by Rizzoli International Publications, Inc.
300 Park Avenue South
New York, NY 10010
www.rizzoliusa.com

Photography by Monica Buck
Designed by Doug Turshen with David Huang

2016 2017 2018 2019 / 10 9 8 7 6 5 4 3 2 1

Distributed in the U.S. trade by Random House, New York

Printed in China

ISBN-13: 978-0-8478-4814-0   33614059720010

Library of Congress Control Number: 2015952938

OPPOSITE: This bouquet of clematis, cosmos, zinnias, agapanthus, and allium
explores the range of purple from deep violet to fuchsia.